Status of Canada Lynx in Voyageurs National Park, Minnesota, 2000-2004

Natural Resource Technical Report NPS/GLKN/NRTR—2009/172

Bill Route
National Park Service
Great Lakes Inventory and Monitoring Network
2800 Lakeshore Drive East, Suite D
Ashland, WI 54806

Steve Windels and Jim Schaberl[1]
National Park Service
Voyageurs National Park
3131 Highway 53 South
International Falls, MN 56649

[1]Current address:
National Park Service
Shenandoah National Park
3655 Hwy 211 East
Luray, VA 22835

February 2009

U.S. Department of the Interior
National Park Service
Natural Resource Program Center
Fort Collins, Colorado

The Natural Resource Publication series addresses natural resource topics that are of interest and applicability to a broad readership in the National Park Service and to others in the management of natural resources, including the scientific community, the public, and the NPS conservation and environmental constituencies. Manuscripts are peer-reviewed to ensure that the information is scientifically credible, technically accurate, appropriately written for the intended audience, and is designed and published in a professional manner.

The Natural Resources Technical Reports series is used to disseminate the peer-reviewed results of scientific studies in the physical, biological, and social sciences for both the advancement of science and the achievement of the National Park Service's mission. The reports provide contributors with a forum for displaying comprehensive data that are often deleted from journals because of page limitations. Current examples of such reports include the results of research that addresses natural resource management issues; natural resource inventory and monitoring activities; resource assessment reports; scientific literature reviews; and peer reviewed proceedings of technical workshops, conferences, or symposia.

Views, statements, findings, conclusions, recommendations and data in this report are solely those of the author(s) and do not necessarily reflect views and policies of the U.S. Department of the Interior, NPS. Mention of trade names or commercial products does not constitute endorsement or recommendation for use by the National Park Service.

Printed copies of reports in these series may be produced in a limited quantity and they are only available as long as the supply lasts. This report is also available from the Natural Resource Publications Management website (http://www.nature.nps.gov/publications/NRPM) on the Internet or by sending a request to the address on the back cover.

Please cite this publication as:

Route, B., S. Windels, and J. Schaberl. 2009. Status of Canada Lynx in Voyageurs National Park, Minnesota, 2000-2004. Natural Resource Technical Report NPS/GLKN/NRTR—2009/172. National Park Service, Fort Collins, Colorado.

NPS D-166, February 2009

Contents

Figures

Tables

Abstract

Between 2000 and 2004 we applied several techniques to determine the presence and status of Canada lynx (*Lynx canadensis*) in Voyageurs National Park, Minnesota. During the winters of 2000-01 and 2001-02 we applied the National Interagency Canada Lynx Detection Protocol (NLDP) with slight modifications. Over the two winters we placed a total of 250 hair snares along transects and checked them twice at approximately 14-day intervals for a combined total of 7,045 exposure days. These hair snares resulted in no lynx detections. Three sets of cat-like snow-tracks were followed and measured during NLDP surveys, but genetic material was not collected. One snow-track met all lynx measurement criteria while the remaining two were inconclusive. After completing two years of NLDP surveys, we verified one male and one female lynx in the park by following incidentally-located snow-tracks until hair or feces were obtained for genetic fingerprinting. We conclude that lynx were present in the park during this time period, but at very low density.

Acknowledgments

We would like to thank A. Dietz, C. Cowden, M. Broschart, and J. Fox for their efforts in the field; U. Gafvert and S. Pratt for assistance with GIS; M. Hyslop for database design; the USFS Eastern Region, Superior National Forest, and Rocky Mountain Research Station Genetics Lab for assistance, supplies, and advice; E. Lindquist, who coordinated the lynx surveys in the Eastern Region of the USFS; and E. Beever, J. Belant, C. Burdett, E. Lindquist, and S. Sanders for helpful comments on earlier drafts of this report.

Introduction

In March 2000, the United States Fish and Wildlife Service (USFWS) listed Canada lynx (*Lynx canadensis*) as "threatened" in the contiguous United States under the Endangered Species Act (USFWS 2000). The USFWS found a paucity of information on the distribution and abundance of lynx and determined that there was a lack of guidance and planning for lynx survival on federal lands. Under Section 7 of the Endangered Species Act, federal agencies, including the National Park Service (NPS), must consult with the USFWS to ensure that their actions do not jeopardize the continued existence of listed species. Section 7 consultations rely on current knowledge of the species' presence, distribution, and abundance on the managed lands.

In anticipation of lynx being listed, the United States Forest Service (USFS), USFWS, Bureau of Land Management, and NPS began developing lynx conservation plans and studies to determine the status of lynx on their lands (Ruediger et al. 2000). As part of this effort an interagency team developed the "National Interagency Lynx Detection Protocol" (NLDP; McKelvey et al. 1999) to help verify the presence of lynx and evaluate their distribution across large areas. The protocol was tested with good results on known lynx populations in Canada and Alaska (McDaniel et al. 2000).

All federal agencies that managed land with potential lynx habitat were invited to use the NLDP in a multi-agency effort from 1999 through 2004 to assess the status of lynx across the northern forested zone of the contiguous United States. To help select survey areas, Ruediger et al. (2000) used coarse-scale habitat assessments and historical trapping records to identify areas with potential for remnant lynx populations. In the Great Lakes region, they identified Voyageurs National Park (VNP) and the Superior National Forest (SNF) in northern Minnesota as areas with high potential for remnant populations. Hence, documenting the presence of lynx became a high priority in those areas.

In 2000 the Ontario Ministry of Natural Resources (OMNR) reported a peak in the Ontario lynx population (OMNR unpublished data). We reasoned that if an invasion were to occur in VNP, it would occur between 2001 and 2004 following the decline phase of the lynx population in Canada (see Appendix A for a brief natural history of the lynx, including its population cycle in north-central North America).

NPS management guidelines call for surveys to determine the distribution and abundance of threatened, endangered, and sensitive species (NPS 1991). A goal of the Great Lakes Inventory and Monitoring Network is to help parks verify species presence and determine the distribution and abundance of species of special concern (Route 2001). Our project objectives were to document the presence and current status of lynx in Voyageurs National Park and to summarize past and current, published and unpublished accounts of lynx within the park and adjacent areas.

Methods

The National Lynx Detection Protocol
The National Lynx Detection Protocol (NLDP) relies on olfactory and visual attractants to lure lynx to a hair snare (McKelvey et al. 1999). The hair snare is laced with catnip to encourage lynx to rub on a piece of carpet studded with short nails and wires that grab hair and attached follicles. The NLDP was designed to provide an unbiased estimate of lynx abundance by placing hair snares across an area in a systematic fashion with a random start. The USFS Eastern Region provided kits with all the snares, lures, and supplies needed to run the survey consistently.

Survey block and anchor point layout
In winter 2000-01 we used a geographic information system (GIS) to pick a random starting point within a 10 km^2 cell in the extreme southeastern corner of VNP. We used that random point to locate a 3.2 km grid across the park's southeast landmass. Grid intercepts became anchor points for transect selection (Figure 1; 2000-01 transects shown as black hash marks). We excluded points that were in open areas >30 m across (i.e., lakes and meadows) or where the total round-trip distance between the access point and the end of the transect was $\geq$4.8 km. The latter criterion helped observers complete one to three transects per day under winter conditions to maintain the 14-day sampling interval required by NLDP. When anchor points could not be sampled, overall sample size was maintained by adding points to the survey grid in a northwesterly direction. The resulting survey block encompassed 209.8 km^2.

Transect orientation
We randomly selected a default compass direction for all transects rather than orienting them "downhill" as stipulated in the NLDP. The NLDP was developed in mountainous terrain in the western United States, and our modification was necessary for the relatively flat topography of north-central Minnesota. A further complication in our study area was the occurrence of numerous openings created by lakes, ponds, and beaver meadows. The NLDP stipulates that openings >30 m are to be crossed and not considered part of the transect; yet, the active transect length must be 400 m and the total distance $\leq$1.5 km. These requirements would have excluded most transects in our study area. To remain unbiased yet allow flexibility in placing transects, we used the following decision rules when a transect could not be kept $\leq$1.5 km:
   a. First, we attempted to slide the transect forward or backward along its axis using the random default bearing until it could be sampled;
   b. If the transect could still not be sampled, we incrementally added 15° to the compass bearing until the transect could be sampled;
   c. If the transect could still not be sampled, the anchor point was excluded and the next point on the grid was selected.

Sampling stations and hair snares
Five stations were placed along each transect at 100 m intervals excluding openings >30 m. This resulted in a total of 125 stations (25 transects with five stations each) in the survey grid. At each station, the nearest tree of sufficient size (>7.6 cm dbh) was selected for a hair snare. The hair

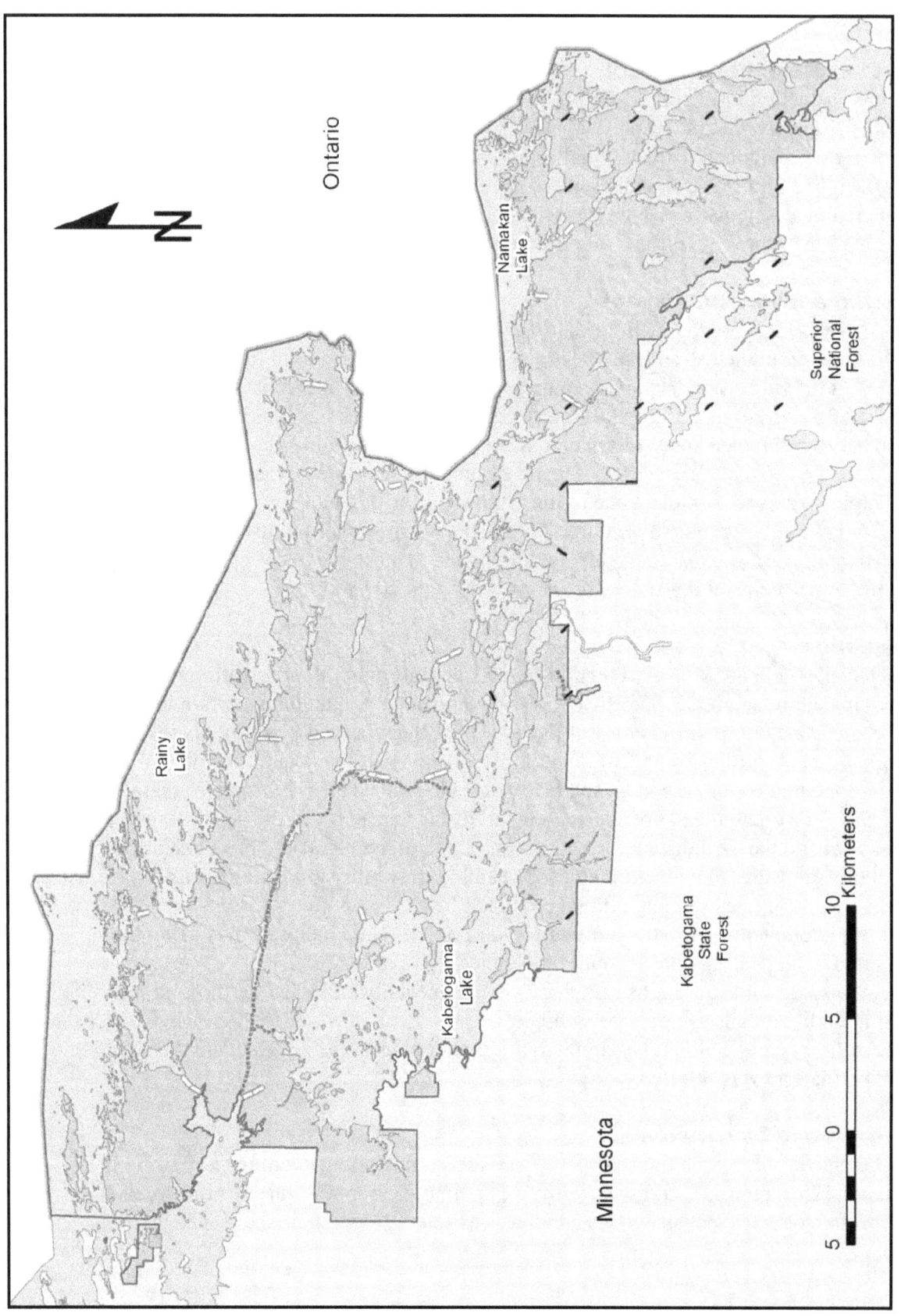

Figure 1. Voyageurs National Park, Minnesota, showing location of NLDP transects (black hash marks = 2000-01; yellow hash marks = 2001-02), snow-tracking routes (red dotted trails), and baiting stations (orange squares) used to document presence of Canada lynx. In the winter of 2000-01 NLDP transects were located in a systematic-random fashion whereas in 2001-02 they were placed in potential lynx travel corridors. Tracking and baiting in the winters of 2002-03 and 2003-04 were conducted opportunistically (see text).

snare was a 16.1-cm2 piece of nail-studded carpet sprinkled with dried catnip to entice lynx to rub it. Within 3 m of the snare, another tree was selected for a combination of visual attractant and scent lure. We used a metal pie plate suspended from a branch as the visual attractant and a 16.1-cm2 piece of carpet anointed with beaver castor, catnip oil, and glycerin (an antifreeze) as the scent lure. All materials, including pie tins, hair snares, and scent lures were provided by the USFS to ensure standardization across all study areas of the northern United States.

Sample handling and DNA analysis

Walking on snowshoes, observers checked each transect twice, separated by approximately 14 days. At each check they looked for hair, repaired/replaced tangled or missing attractants, and added scent lure. Snares believed to have hair were immediately placed in plastic Ziploc™ bags and marked with station number, date, and observer name. Within 12 hours the hair was removed from the pad with tweezers and placed in a vial with desiccant. We sent all hair samples to the USFS Rocky Mountain Research Station in Missoula, MT, for fingerprinting of mitochondrial DNA (mtDNA) to determine species and fingerprinting of nuclear DNA to distinguish between individual lynx (Mills et al. 2000).

Modified NLDP

In winter 2001-02 we abandoned the systematic grid of the NLDP, due to lack of lynx detections. We instead placed transects in forested corridors between lakes and open meadows. Given the mosaic of openings, ponds, and lakes in the study area, we reasoned that these corridors would provide cover in areas where lynx were more likely to travel. While this non-random design limits inference across the study area, it was a reasonable trade-off, given our primary objective of establishing presence.

We used 1:24,000-scale topographic maps and aerial photographs to identify and locate forested corridors between lakes, ponds, and meadows primarily in the northern half of the park (known as the Kabetogama Peninsula), but some in the southeast mainland section, as well. We then chose those corridors that, when linked together with lakes, ponds, and meadows, dissected the peninsula in as many places as possible, given logistical and time constraints. Thus we attempted to maximize the potential for a traveling lynx to encounter a station. We placed 25 transects, in some cases end to end, such that lynx moving along the peninsula would likely walk within 50 m of a station (i.e., the midpoint between standard NLDP stations). As in the previous year, we avoided transects where the total round-trip distance on snowshoes was $\geq$4.8 km (3 mi) so that sampling of all 25 stations could be completed during each of the two 14-day time periods. All other hair-snare methods followed the NLDP, as stated above. The 2001-02 survey was conducted primarily on the 300 km^2 (116 mi^2) Kabetogama Peninsula with a few transects in the southeastern section of the park (Figure 1; 2001-02 transects shown as yellow hash marks).

Snow-tracking

We recorded all carnivore tracks encountered while snowshoeing to and along transects. For tracks that resembled those of lynx, we took standard measurements of stride, group, straddle, and footprint length at three locations along the animal's trail where prints were clearest (Halfpenny et al. 1995). Observers were experienced biologists and fur trappers who, prior to the survey, were trained in the methods of measuring tracks. Each observer was provided with calipers, a ruler, camera, and standard forms.

We used discriminant analysis on mean track measurements to distinguish between bobcat, lynx, and mountain lion (Halfpenny et al. 1995: 103). We also compared the average and range of measurements with known tracks of lynx, bobcat, and mountain lion (Halfpenny et al. 1995; J. Halfpenny unpublished data; D. Loch unpublished data).

Opportunistic surveys and baiting

During the winters of 2002-03 and 2003-04, VNP staff conducted opportunistic snow-tracking surveys and baiting (Figure 1; red dotted trails and orange squares). This included non-standardized track surveys along established snowmobile routes and ski/snowshoe trails when snow conditions and staff time allowed. In 2002-03, a single hair snare was set near fresh bait near the Rainy Lake Visitor Center and visited approximately weekly through March. In winter 2003-04, VNP staff maintained two bait stations, the same one near the Rainy Lake Visitor Center and another near the Ash River Visitor Center. The stations were baited with deer or beaver meat and a scent lure (Gusto™) and were visited weekly from February 7 through March 26, 2004. Bait and attractant were added as necessary during each visit.

In addition to conducting active and passive surveys for lynx, we recorded reports of observations from the public and other natural resource professionals and investigated them when possible.

Results

Standard and modified NLDP

Using standard and modified versions of the NLDP, we placed 250 hair snares for lynx in VNP during the winters of 2000-01 and 2001-02. Snares were left out for an average of 28 days (range 26-31 days), for a total of 7,045 snare-days. On average, hair snares were checked and re-lured 14 days after placement (range 12-15 days).

The snares were successful at obtaining hair on only six occasions (Table 1). Of these, two could not be sequenced due to an inadequate amount of hair or poor quality of DNA. Another hair sample could not be identified to species because the lab lacked reference DNA. Two hair samples were identified as white-tailed deer (*Odocoileus virginianus*), and one was identified as either a wolf (*Canis lupus*) or domestic dog (*C. familiaris*).

White-tailed deer are common in the VNP area, and their hair is ubiquitous in the forest. We found no evidence of deer rubbing on snares (no tracks in the snow). While tracks could have been obliterated by weather, it is likely that the hair was deposited by the wind. Wolves are also fairly common in the VNP area (Gogan et al. 2005). It is not currently possible to differentiate wolves and dogs by DNA analysis of hair; however, because the snare location was far from any human establishment, it is likely that the hair was from a wolf.

Table 1. Results of hair sample fingerprinting. Samples were sent to the USFS Genetics Laboratory in Missoula, MT, where they were subjected to DNA extraction and amplification (Mills et al. 2000) as part of a nationwide protocol to detect Canada lynx in northern forested areas.

Date	Transect	Station	Result
3/10/2001	2	5	White-tailed deer
3/28/2001	30	3	White-tailed deer
3/1/2002	3	4	Poor DNA sample[1]
3/2/2002	17	5	Wolf or dog[2]
3/14/2002	5	1	Poor DNA sample[1]
3/15/2002	4	2	Species unknown[3]

[1]Nationally, about 20-30% of all DNA could not be amplified to the species level.
[2]Wolves and domestic dogs cannot be differentiated using standard DNA amplification techniques.
[3]Quality DNA but species could not be identified due to a lack of comparable genetic material.

Snow-tracking

While conducting the NLDP during the winters of 2000-01 and 2001-02, we walked 60 km (37.5 mi) of active transect by snowshoe. We did not record the distance to the start of each active transect, which was up to 1.1 km from a snowmobile, nor did we record kilometers of snowmobile routes traveled to where the snowmobile was parked to access each transect. Hence the actual distance surveyed was likely much larger than 60 km. We encountered and measured three sets of tracks (0.012 tracks per km of transect) that were characteristic of a large cat (i.e., four clawless toes on a round foot print >8 cm in size; see Table 2). Using the discriminant techniques developed by Halfpenny et al. (1995), all three tracks scored above the suggested threshold for bobcat and below the threshold for mountain lion. We also compared these measurements with other known lynx tracks and tracking guides (Halfpenny and Biesiot 1986; Halfpenny et al. 1995; J.C. Halfpenny, unpublished data; S. Loch, unpublished data).

The tracks encountered on transect 18, station 4 are consistent with all sources of lynx track measurements (Table 2; Figure 2). This track was encountered approximately 5 km (3 mi) southwest of VNP near Big Johnson Lake in the Superior National Forest. The tracks were old, but several prints were measurable, and the stride, group, and straddle are durable even in poor snow conditions. We conclude that these tracks were from a lynx. We are less certain about the other two tracks even though they met the threshold for lynx in the discriminant analysis. These tracks had short strides and small footprints for lynx at this time of year (i.e., even juvenile lynx should be nearly adult-sized), but see Discussion section below.

Opportunistic surveys and baiting

We spent approximately 100 person-hours intermittently searching for lynx tracks, feces, and hair during the winters of 2002-03 and 2003-04. Roughly 20% of the combined effort was spent in 2003-04 monitoring a 1.6-km stretch of snowshoe trail near the Ash River Visitor Center on a weekly basis throughout winter. Approximately half of this effort occurred on March 2, 2004, when seven NPS employees and volunteers searched along the Chain of Lakes snowmobile trail that bisects the Kabetogama Peninsula. The remainder of the effort was on intermittent surveys along the Chain of Lakes trail throughout March 2004.

As a result of these intermittent surveys a set of tracks, hair, and feces was found on March 9, 2004, south of Shoepack Lake on the Kabetogama Peninsula (Figure 2). The hair and feces were sent to the USFS genetics lab and subsequently verified as coming from a female lynx.

Hair snares were set near fresh bait and lure for approximately 20-30 days during March 2003 and for 47 days during late February and March 2004. No lynx activity was detected at bait stations, although fishers and wolves were frequent visitors.

Table 2. Summary information and measurements for probable lynx tracks observed during surveys in Voyageurs National Park, MN, 2000-2002. All averages from 2001 reflect measurements of three separate prints; the range of the measures is shown in parentheses except where noted.

| Date | Site | Station | Species | Tracker comments | Average and range of measurements (cm) | | | Front footprint | |
					Stride	Group	Straddle	Length	Width
3/24/2001	18	4	Lynx	Poor tracking conditions but tracks measurable. Animal stayed on top of snow and walked along snow covered windfalls; had a staggered walk rather than a straight line. Tracks round.	77.7 (71-81)	43.6 (30-61)	21 (18-25)	11.5 (11.5-11.5)	11.5 (11.5-11.5)
3/10/2001	2	5	Unknown	Snow in tracks but measurable. Pie tin visited by animal, but hair snare 10 feet away, was not. Animal stayed up on snow and walked on wind-fallen trees. Direct registry of tracks may have caused slight elongation of footprint.	51.3 (49-55)	34.7 (34-35.5)	20.5 (19-22.5)	9.1 (8.5-9.5)	8.8 (8.5-9.0)
3/10/2001	4	4	Unknown	Circled the pie tin and tree with scent pad. Stayed up on snow and exhibited cat-like behavior. Direct registry of tracks may have caused slight elongation of footprint.	58.3 (57-60)	40 (38.5-41.5)	20 (17-23)	9.1 (8.5-9.7)	8.9 (8.7-9.2)
Known track measurements for comparison: (Halfpenny et al. 1995; J. Halfpenny, unpublished data; S. Loch, unpublished data).				Bobcat	56.0		12.7	5.0	5.0
				Juvenile lynx	68.1 (58-90.1)	42.1 (36.5-53.3)	15 (12.5-23.5)	7.2 (6.4-8.4)	9.4 (8.8-10.8)
*Standard deviation				Adult lynx	77.3 (72-84)	48.6 (44.2-53.5)	21.2 (17.6-24.8)*	10 (8.5-11.5)	10 (8.8-11.5)
				Cougar	102		20.3	9.0	9.0

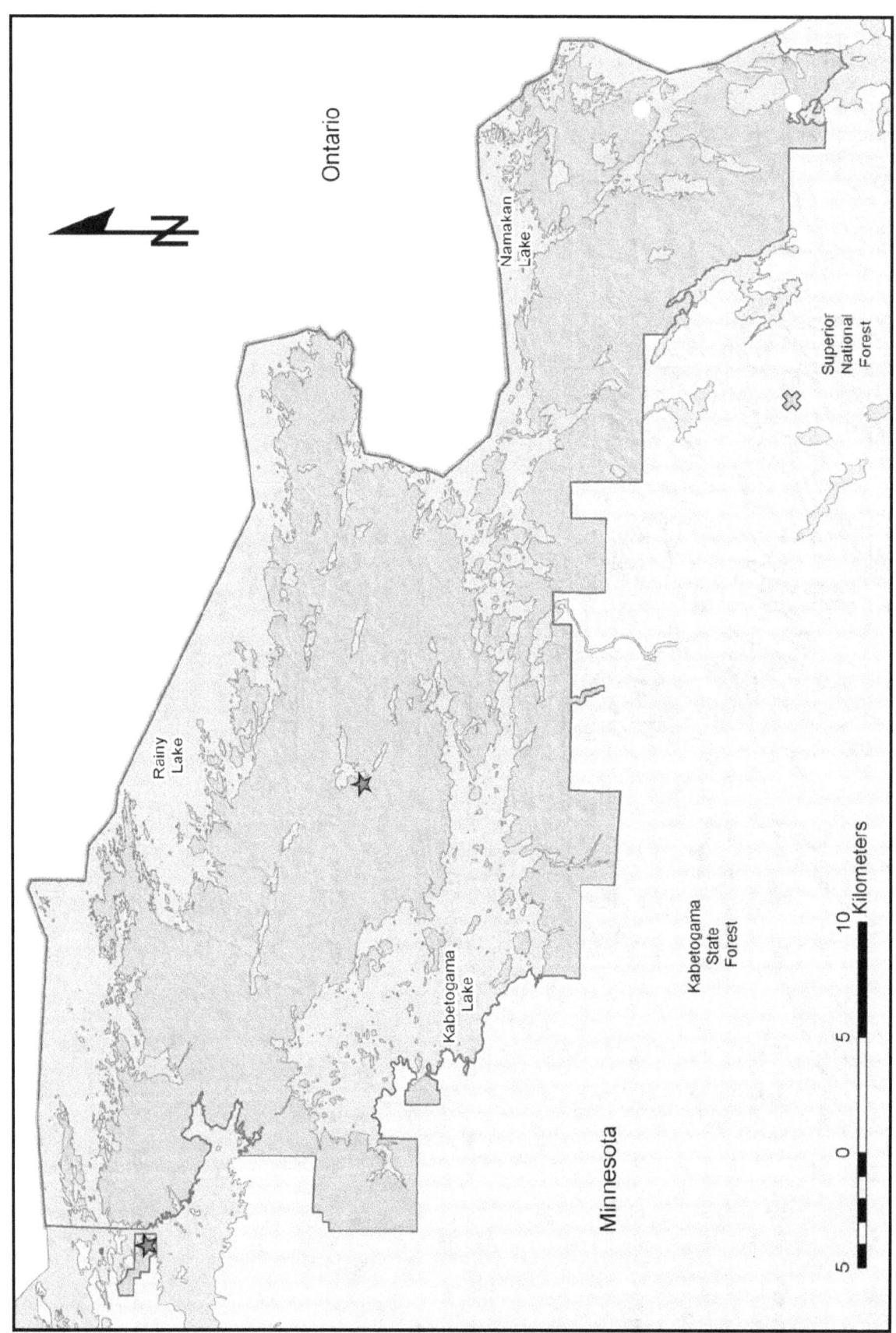

Figure 2. Voyageurs National Park, Minnesota, showing locations where Canada lynx were verified by DNA from hair and scat collected along snow-tracks (red stars) or reliable snow-tracks (orange cross). Also shown are the locations of two snow-tracks that were consistent with lynx except for the stride, which was midway in size between lynx and bobcat (yellow dots).

Anecdotal observations

In March 2003 a VNP employee inadvertently came across tracks of a large cat near the Rainy Lake Visitor Center. The tracks were subsequently followed by two NPS biologists who found feces. The feces were sent to the USFS lab and verified by DNA extraction as coming from a male lynx. This finding was the first verification of a Canada lynx within the boundaries of Voyageurs National Park in recent history (Figure 2).

We recorded nine other incidental sightings by the public of potential lynx or lynx sign within 56 km (35 mi) of VNP (Table 3). Six of these were visual observations of lynx, and three others were tracks. We have high confidence in five of these reports, based on the observers' experience and the supporting information, but we cannot be certain. A video was reportedly taken of a lynx in February 2002 at Island View Resort. This video could not be corroborated because NPS employees were refused access. This potential lynx sighting is within 2 km (1.25 mi) of the lynx verified by DNA the following year near the Rainy Lake Visitor Center.

Table 3. Anecdotal observations of Canada lynx reported to the National Park Service between 2000 and 2003 in and adjacent to Voyageurs National Park, MN.

| Date of observation | Type of detection | Location | Distance from nearest edge of study area | | Confidence |
			mi	km	
Feb-00	Visual	Dryden, ON	35	56	Moderate
10-Feb-01	Visual	Atikokan, ON	35	56	Moderate
12-Feb-01	Visual	Ray, MN	4	6.5	High
13-Feb-01	Visual	S. of Dryden, ON	25	40	High
Feb-01	Tracks	Ray, MN	4	6.5	High
Feb-01	Visual	Kabetogama, MN	2	3	High
Mar-01	Tracks	W. of Kabetogama, MN	2	3	Moderate
Feb-02	Video	Island View, MN	2	3	Moderate
Mar-02	Tracks	Ray, MN	4	6.5	High
Mar-03	Tracks	Rainy Lake Visitor Center	In	In	Confirmed*

*These tracks were followed to feces that were collected and subsequently verified by DNA as coming from a male lynx.

Discussion

We were unsuccessful at detecting lynx using original and modified versions of the NLDP during the winters of 2000-01 and 2001-02 respectively, but our results were not unlike other studies in the Great Lakes region (Table 4). From 1999 through 2003, 525 transects consisting of 2,625 hair snare stations (approximately 73,500 hair-snare exposure days) resulted in no lynx being detected across six federal land management units in the Great Lakes region. It is possible that lynx were either: 1) non-existent, 2) at extremely low densities, 3) distributed in a manner that was incompatible with the NLDP, or 4) undetected because the NLDP and modified versions were ineffective in winter. McDaniel et al. (2000) have shown success with the NLDP during snow-free periods in the western United States, albeit in moderate- to high-density lynx populations. However, Moen et al. (2004a) followed a radio-collared lynx during winter in northern Minnesota that went undetected as it passed through an NLDP survey grid. They then added five additional transects to the NLDP grid to encompass fully the home range of the radio-collared lynx. This lynx remained undetected by the NLDP method. Further research indicated that home ranges of at least two other radio-collared lynx overlapped the grid and that as many as five lynx may have been in the area (Burdett et al. 2006).

We considered possible problems with the effectiveness of the attractants and lures in winter. Investigators in Alaska and Canada have used beaver castor and glycerin to capture hundreds of lynx during very cold (to -25°F) winter weather (Route and Doyle 1991; Mowat et al. 1996). Fur trappers across Alaska and Canada trap during winter when pelts are in prime condition. They use a variety of visual attractants, including pie tins, and combine them with scent lures such as beaver castor with glycerin to keep the scent active in cold weather (B. Route, personal observation). While it is possible that the lures used in the NLDP are less volatile in winter compared to summer, we have no reason to believe they were ineffective at bringing lynx to the detection site. Rather, we suspect that the final step in the NLDP of enticing lynx to rub on the hair-snare using catnip was of greater concern for winter use. Based on three sets of cat tracks noted at the NLDP stations in our study, apparently two cats circled the pie plates, but did not rub on the hair snare.

Developers of the NLDP exposed a captive lynx to catnip-laced snares and documented extensive rubbing behavior on video (video reviewed by B. Route and available from J. Halfpenny). However, to our knowledge, this type of trial was not performed in winter. It is possible that the scent of catnip does not carry well during cold weather or is not of interest to lynx at that time of year. Schmidt and Kowalczyk (2006) suggest that the European lynx (*Lynx lynx*) may be more inclined to rub during the breeding season than at other times of the year. March is the breeding season for lynx in North America, and most of the lynx activity we detected occurred at that time. Yet catnip is not a scent that is normally associated with lynx mating behavior, and it may have been ineffective at enticing them to rub. Potentially, cat urine or anal gland oil would have been more effective.

Table 4. Results of efforts by the National Forest Service, the Natural Resources Research Institute, and this study to verify the occurrence of Canada lynx with the National Lynx Detection Protocol on federal lands in the Great Lakes region. Data are from Moen et al. (2004) for surveys on National Forest (NF) lands and from this study for National Park (NP) lands.

Year	Season	Area Surveyed	No. of Transects	Verifications from DNA
1999	Fall	Superior NF, MN	25	0
1999	Fall	Nicolet NF, MI	25	0
1999	Fall	Ottawa NF, MI	25	0
1999-2000	Winter	Superior NF, MN	25	0
1999-2000	Winter	Chequamegon NF, WI	25	0
1999-2000	Winter	Chippewa NF, MN	25	0
2000	Fall	Chequamegon NF, WI	25	1 bobcat
2000-2001	Winter	Superior NF, MN	75	0
2000-2001	Winter	Ottawa NF, MI	25	1 bobcat
2000-2001	Winter	Chippewa NF, MN	25	4 bobcat[1]
2000-2001	Winter	Voyageurs NP, MN	25	0
2001	Fall	Chequamegon NF, WI	25	1 bobcat
2001-2002	Winter	Superior NF, MN	50	2 bobcat[1]
2001-2002	Winter	Ottawa NF, MI	25	0
2001-2002	Winter	Chippewa NF, MN	25	0
2001-2002	Winter	Voyageurs NP, MN[2]	25	0
2002-2003	Winter	Superior NF, MN	25	0
2003	Summer	Superior NF, MN[3]	25	0
		Total transects:	525	-
		Total detections:	Lynx	0
			Bobcat	9

[1]Multiple bobcat detections on one forest may indicate a single animal.
[2]Survey did not follow the traditional NLDP methods (see text).
[3]Survey grid was known to encompass home range(s) of >1 lynx (Moen et al. 2004a).

In our study, two of six (33%) hair samples could not be sequenced. Nationally, about 20% to 30% of all hair samples sent for DNA testing as part of the NLDP could not be sequenced due to poor quality DNA, and preliminary findings suggest this rate is greatest in studies conducted in winter (K. Pilgrim, USFS geneticist, personal communication). Frequent collections and careful handling of DNA material is essential in future studies.

We verified the presence of at least two lynx in VNP after collecting hair or feces for DNA fingerprinting. Track surveys in winter, when they included following trails until genetic material was found, were more effective at detecting lynx than passive methods such as using lures and baits (see also Burdett et al. 2006; McKelvey et al. 2006).

When time or other logistical concerns precludes finding genetic material, then careful measurements of the tracks can be diagnostic. Of the three tracks that we measured we were reasonably confident that one was a lynx, but the other two remain unknown. The footprints and straddle of these unknown tracks were too large for a bobcat and within the range of a small adult lynx, but the stride and group measurements were short compared to known averages for a walking lynx. Interestingly, in northeastern Minnesota, of 20 'lynx' DNA samples sent for genetic verification, three (15%) were found to be genetic hybrids between male bobcats and female lynx (Schwartz et al. 2004). Taxonomically similar species whose ranges overlap are known to occasionally hybridize, especially when the population of one species is swamped by the other. The bobcat's range has moved north in concert with increased forest fragmentation and warmer winters with dense snow packs (Buskirk et al. 2000). The lynx/bobcat hybrids reported by Schwartz et al. (2004) in Minnesota are the first known occurrences of bobcat and lynx hybridization. Reportedly, a fourth hybrid was observed on Sand Point Island in Ontario, Canada, northwest of our study area, and a possible fifth has been found in Wisconsin (A. Wydeven, personal communication).

In the three hybrid specimens found dead in Minnesota (Schwartz et al. 2004), the legs were slightly shorter and the feet were smaller than those of a pure lynx (E. Lindquist, personal communication). The short legs and medium-sized foot pads of a hybrid could account for the inconsistent stride, group, and foot measurements of the two unknown tracks that we encountered in March 2001 (Table 2; Figure 2). These tracks could have been from a single individual, given their proximity in time and space. However, this conjecture would require further evidence to be substantiated.

Status of lynx in the region

Statewide, the Minnesota Department of Natural Resources (MNDNR) recorded 263 sightings of lynx or lynx sign from March 2000, when they were first listed as federally threatened, through mid-November 2004 (Figure 3). Of these, 130 (49%) were verified by MNDNR personnel, and 10 (7.7%) of these included evidence of reproduction (tracks or visual observations of juveniles). These sightings are not the result of a systematic effort on the part of the MNDNR. They are incidental encounters reported by natural resource professionals as well as by the public, so they tend to cluster along roads and other places frequented by people. While these sightings help delineate a coarse geographic range of lynx in Minnesota, they say very little about remote areas such as VNP and cannot be used to estimate lynx abundance.

Some of the sightings documented by MNDNR (Figure 3) are the result of an intensive investigation by researchers from the Natural Resources Research Institute (NRRI) and the Biological Resources Division of the U.S. Geological Survey (USGS) in eastern portions of the Superior National Forest (SNF; Moen et al. 2004a, 2004b). The NRRI and USGS investigators conducted NLDP surveys from 1999 through 2003 with no lynx detections (Table 4); however, in 2001 they followed a set of incidental tracks to a day-bed and found hair, which was subsequently verified as coming from a lynx. The investigators began more extensive track surveys and documented several lynx in eastern portions of the SNF and Boundary Waters Canoe Area Wilderness. They began live-trapping and radio-collaring lynx in February 2003, and by the end of December 2004 they had trapped and radio-collared 17 adult and one subadult lynx, including nine females and nine males (Figure 4; Moen et al. 2004b).

The NRRI/USGS study is currently documenting reproduction, movement patterns, home-range size, habitat characteristics, and prey availability for lynx in northeastern Minnesota. Thus far, most collared lynx have remained in extreme northeastern Minnesota and southern Ontario,

Canada (Figure 4). One individual has been located as far west as Little Fork, Minnesota, which is approximately 80 km (48 mi) south of the VNP boundary.

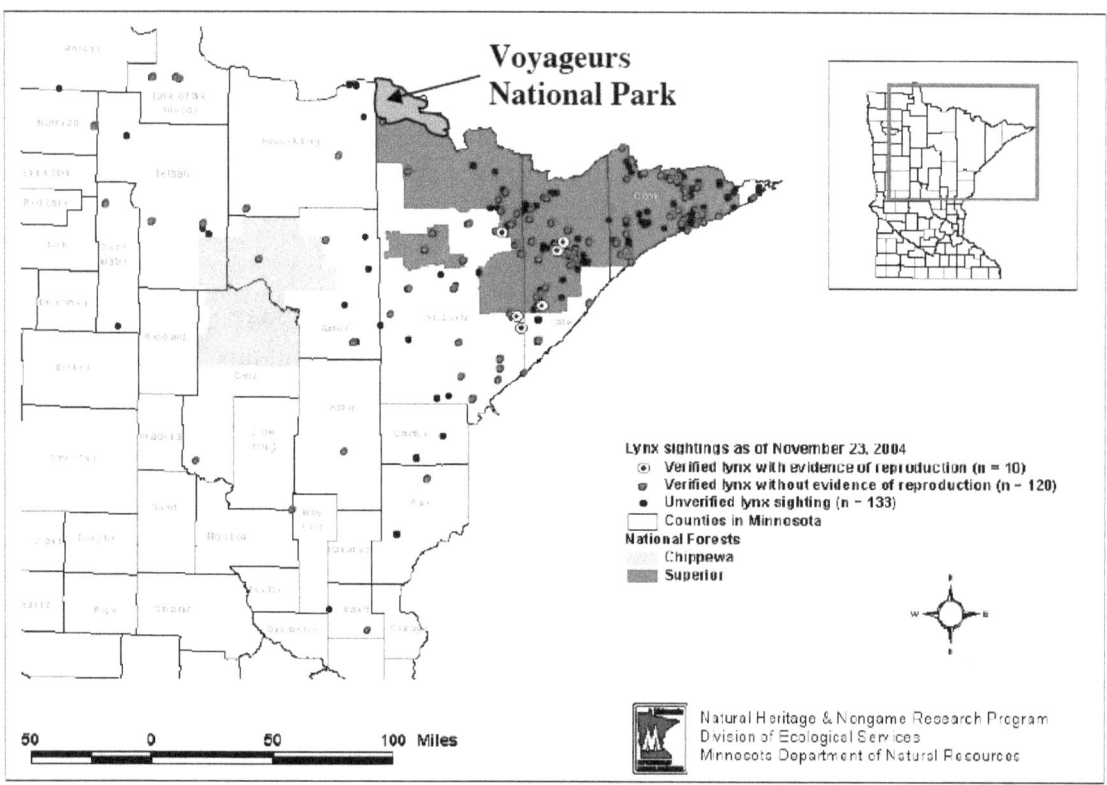

Figure 3. Sightings of Canada lynx that were reported to the Minnesota Department of Natural Resources between March 2000 and November 2004 (MNDNR 2004).

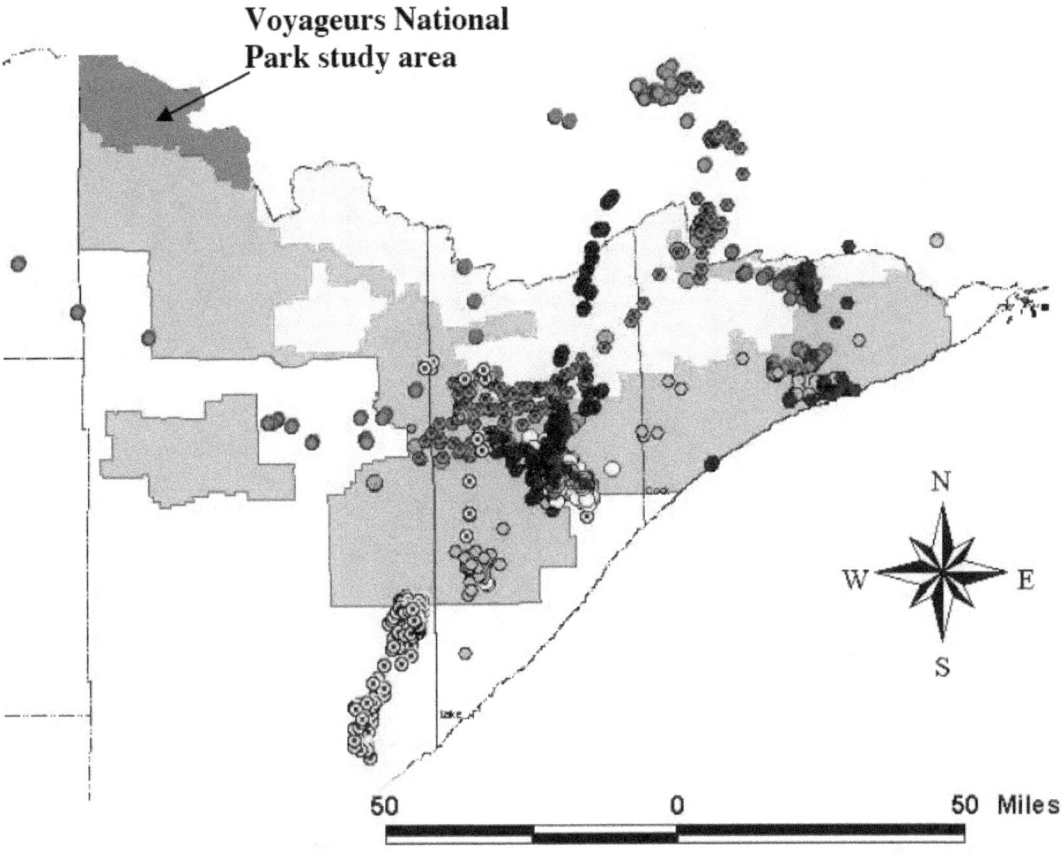

Figure 4. Locations of Canada lynx radio-collared south and east of Voyageurs National Park. Different colored circles depict different lynx. The Superior National Forest is shown in orange and the Boundary Waters Canoe Area Wilderness in light green. Data are from Moen et al. (2004b).

Conclusions and Recommendations

- We used DNA fingerprinting to document at least one male and one female lynx within VNP during the winters of 2003 and 2004, respectively. Snow-tracking by project investigators and incidental sightings by the public, while not conclusive, suggest lynx were present in the immediate area as early as 2000. Collection of this evidence required considerable effort, both in systematic and opportunistic surveys. Hence we conclude that lynx were either transient or present at a low density.

- Lynx and bobcat hybridization is occurring in the Great Lakes region and possibly in VNP. Hybridization between male bobcats and female lynx has been documented near VNP (Schwartz et al. 2004), and we may have encountered tracks of such an animal within park boundaries. The effects of hybridization on lynx conservation in the region are not fully understood.

- The National Lynx Detection Protocol (NLDP) has thus far proven unsuccessful at detecting lynx in the Great Lakes region. The objective of the NLDP was to provide an unbiased estimate of lynx presence/absence across the forested region of the conterminous United States. At the management unit level, the systematic placement of NLDP transects is less efficient than more focused efforts to find tracks and follow them for DNA verification. This conclusion is based on results of our study and efforts by Burdett et al. (2006) and McKelvey et al. (2006). Where possible, any additional efforts at VNP should be directed at extensive and timely surveys to locate and then follow tracks to locate hair or scat for DNA verification (see McKelvey et al. 2006).

- Snow-tracking is a reasonable means of documenting wildlife when DNA verification is not possible (Halfpenny et al. 1995; Wydeven et al. 1999). However, track surveys should be completed within 24 to 48 hours after a fresh snow, when tracks have had time to accumulate yet are still easily identified. Early in this study, our survey methods were tied to the NLDP with a pre-set number of days between visits. Hence, tracks that we encountered were sometimes old and degraded by snow, sun, and wind.

- Two of the most pressing questions regarding lynx conservation in Minnesota and the other Great Lakes states are: 1) whether Canada lynx are successfully breeding and reproducing, and 2) whether Canada lynx are persisting during lows in the population cycle. Research by Moen et al. (2004*a*, 2004*b*) on population status, movements, and reproduction of a small population of lynx in northeastern Minnesota will hopefully begin to answer these questions. At a minimum, VNP biologists should continue to track lynx opportunistically and follow them until samples of hair and/or feces can be found for genetic fingerprinting. If funds and time allow, areas found to be inhabited by lynx should be trapped, and any lynx that are captured should be radio-monitored to determine if reproduction is occurring through time.

Literature Cited

Aubrey, K. B., G. Koehler, and J. R. Squires. 2000. Ecology of Canada lynx in southern boreal forests. Pages 373-396 *in* L. F. Ruggiero, K. B. Aubrey, S. W. Buskirk, G. M. Koehler, C. J. Krebs, K. S. McKelvey, and J. R. Squires, editors. Ecology and conservation of lynx in the United States. University Press of Colorado, Boulder.

Brand, C. J., and L. B. Keith. 1979. Lynx demography during a snowshoe hare decline in Alberta. Journal of Wildlife Management **43**:827-849.

Burdett, C., E. Lindquist, R. Moen, J. Niemi, and B. Route. 2006. National interagency Canada lynx detection survey in Minnesota, Wisconsin, and Michigan. Technical Report No. NRRI/TR-2006-29. University of Minnesota, Natural Resources Research Institute, Duluth.

Buskirk, S. W., L. F. Ruggiero, and C. J. Krebs. 2000. Habitat fragmentation and interspecific competition: Implications for lynx conservation. Pages 83-100 *in* L. F. Ruggiero, K. B. Aubrey, S. W. Buskirk, G. M. Koehler, C. J. Krebs, K. S. McKelvey, and J. R. Squires, editors. Ecology and conservation of lynx in the United States. University Press of Colorado, Boulder.

Gogan, J. P., W. T. Route, E. M. Olexa, N. Thomas, D. Kuehn, and K. M. Proruzny. 2005. Gray wolves in and adjacent to Voyageurs National Park, Minnesota – Research and synthesis 1987-1991. Technical Report NPS/MWR/NRTR/ 2004-01. U.S. Department of the Interior, National Park Service, Midwest Regional Office, Omaha, NE.

Halfpenny, J. C., and E. Biesiot. 1986. A Field Guide to Mammal Tracking in North America. Johnson Printing, Boulder, CO.

Halfpenny, J. C., R. W. Thompson, S. C. Morse, T. Holden, and P. Rezendes. 1995. Snow tracking. Pages 91-163 *in* W. J. Zielinski and T. E. Kucera, editors. American marten, fisher, lynx, and wolverine: Survey methods for their detection. General Technical Report PSW-GTR-157, USDA Forest Service, Albany, CA.

Hodges, K. E. 2000. Ecology of snowshoe hares in southern boreal and montane forests. Chapter 7 *in* L. F. Ruggiero, K. B. Aubrey, S. W. Buskirk, G. M. Koehler, C. J. Krebs, K. S. McKelvey, and J. R. Squires, editors. Ecology and conservation of lynx in the United States. University Press of Colorado, Boulder.

Kohler, G. M., and K. B. Aubrey. 1994. Chapter 4 – Lynx. Pages 74-98 *in* L. F. Ruggiero, K. B. Aubry, S. W. Buskirk, L. J. Lyon, and W. J. Zielinski, editors. The scientific basis for conserving forest carnivores: American marten, fisher, lynx, and wolverine in the western United States. General Technical Report RM-254. USDA Forest Service, Rocky Mountain Forest and Range Experiment Station, Fort Collins, CO.

McCord, C. M., and J. E. Cardoza. 1982. Bobcat and lynx. Pages 728-766 *in* J. A. Chapman and G. A. Feldhammer, editors. Wild mammals of North America. Johns Hopkins University Press, Baltimore, MD.

McDaniel, G. W., K. S. McKelvey, J. R. Squires, and L. F. Ruggerio. 2000. Efficacy of lures and hair snares to detect lynx. 2000 Wildlife Society Bulletin **28**:119-123.

McKelvey, K. S., J. J. Claar, G. W. McDaniel, and G. Hanvey. 1999. National lynx detection protocol. Unpublished survey protocol. United States Forest Service, Rocky Mountain Research Station, Missoula, MT.

McKelvey, K. S., J. Von Kienast, K. B. Aubrey, G. M. Koehler, B. T. Maletzke, J. R. Squires, E. L. Lindquist, S. Loch, and M. K. Schwartz. 2006. DNA analysis of hair and scat collected along snow tracks to document the presence of Canada lynx. Wildlife Society Bulletin **34**:451-455.

McKelvey, K. S., K. B. Aubrey, and Y. K. Ortega. 2000. History and distribution of lynx in the contiguous United States. Pages 207-264 *in* L. F. Ruggiero, K. B. Aubrey, S. W. Buskirk, G. M. Koehler, C. J. Krebs, K. S. McKelvey, and J. R. Squires, editors. Ecology and conservation of lynx in the United States. University Press of Colorado, Boulder.

Mech, L. D. 1973. Canadian lynx invasion of Minnesota. Biological Conservation **5**:151-152.

Mech, L. D. 1977. Record movement of a Canada lynx. Journal of Mammalogy **58**:676-677.

Mech L. D. 1980. Age, sex, reproduction, and spatial organization of lynxes colonizing northeastern Minnesota. Journal of Mammalogy **61**:261-267.

Mills, L. S., K. L. Pilgrim, M. K. Schwartz, and K. S. McKelvey. 2000. Identifying lynx and other North American felids based on MtDNA analysis. Conservation Genetics **1**:285-288.

Minnesota Department of Natural Resources (MNDNR). 2004. Lynx sightings. Minnesota Department of Natural Resources, Ecological Services. (Online). www.dnr.state.mn.us/ecological_services/nhnrp/research/lynx_sightings.html. Accessed November 2004.

Moen, R., G. Niemi, C. L. Burdett, and L. D. Mech. 2004a. Canada lynx in the Great Lakes region. 2003 annual report to the USDA Forest Service and the Minnesota Cooperative Fish and Wildlife Research Unit. Natural Resources Research Institute Technical Report No. NRRI/TR-2004-01. University of Minnesota, Natural Resources Research Institute, Duluth.

Moen, R., G. Niemi, C. L. Burdett, and L. D. Mech. 2004b. Canada lynx in the Great Lakes region. 2004 annual report to the USDA Forest Service and the Minnesota Cooperative Fish and Wildlife Research Unit. Natural Resources Research Institute Technical Report

No. NRRI/TR-2004-33. University of Minnesota, Natural Resources Research Institute, Duluth.

Mowat, G., B. G. Slough, and S. Boutin. 1996. Lynx recruitment during a snowshoe hare population peak and decline in southwest Yukon. Journal of Wildlife Management **60**:441-452.

National Park Service (NPS). 1991. Natural resources management guideline. U.S. Department of the Interior, National Park Service. Management Policy 77.

O'Donoghue, M., S. Boutin, C. J. Krebs, G. Zuleta, D. L. Murray, and E. J. Hofer. 1998. Functional responses of coyotes and lynx to the snowshoe hare cycle. Ecology **79**:1193-1208.

Quinn, N. W. S., and G. Parker. 1987. Chapter 51 – Lynx. Pages 682-695 *in* M. Novak, J. A. Baker, M. E. Obbard, and B. Malloch, editors. Wild furbearer management and conservation in North America. Ministry of Natural Resources, Ontario, Canada.

Route, B. 2001. Study plan for conducting biological inventories: FY 2001-2004. U.S. Department of the Interior, National Park Service. Great Lakes Inventory and Monitoring Network, Ashland, WI.

Route, B., and T. Doyle. 1991. Mortality factors, home range characteristics, and habitat preferences of lynx inhabiting Tetlin National Wildlife Refuge and Wrangell-St. Elias National Park and Preserve, Alaska. WRST-RM Report No. 91-01. Wrangell-St. Elias National Park and Preserve, Glennallen, AK.

Ruediger, B., J. Caar, S. Gnaidek, B. Holt, L. Lewis, S. Myghton, B. Naney, G. Patton, T. Rinaldi, J. Trick, A. Vandehey, F. Wahl, N. Warren, D. Wenger, and A. Williamson. 2000. Canada lynx conservation assessment and strategy. Forest Service Publication #R1-00-53. USDA Forest Service, USDI Fish and Wildlife Service, USDI Bureau of Land Management, and USDI National Park Service, Missoula, MT.

Schmidt, K. and R. Kowalczyk. 2006. Using scent-marking stations to collect hair samples to monitor Eurasian lynx populations. Wildlife Society Bulletin **34**:462-466.

Schwartz, M. K., K. L. Pilgrim, K. S. McKelvey, E. L. Lindquist, J .J. Claar, and S. Loch. 2004. Hybridization between Canada lynx and bobcats: Genetic results and management implications. Conservation Genetics **5**:349-355.

U. S. Fish and Wildlife Service (USFWS). 2000. Final Rule: Determination of threatened status for the contiguous U.S. distinct population segment of the Canada lynx and related rule. Federal Register **65**:16052-16086.

Ward, R. M. P., and C. J. Krebs. 1985. Behavioral response of lynx to declining snowshoe hare abundance. Canadian Journal of Zoology **63**:2817-2824.

Wydeven, A. P., J. E. Wiedenhoeft, B. E. Kohn, R. P. Thiel, R. N. Schultz, and S. R. Boles. 1999. Progress report of wolf population monitoring in Wisconsin for the period October 1998-March 1999. Unpublished report. Wisconsin Department of Natural Resources, Park Falls, WI.

Appendix. A brief natural history of the Canada lynx in the Great Lakes region.

Canada lynx are medium-sized cats that inhabit northern and southern boreal forests where cold, snowy winters prevail. Adult lynx weigh 8-11.6 kg (18-25.5 lb) and have long legs and large paws adapted for hunting on snow (Figure 1). In the more southerly and warmer reaches of their range, such as the Great Lakes region, compaction of snow and the formation of crust may reduce the competitive advantage that lynx have over bobcat (*Lynx rufus*) and coyote (*Canis latrans*). Buskirk et al. (2000) found that direct exploitation by coyotes and competition with coyotes and bobcat were potentially important factors in lynx abundance.

Eighty-eight percent of the documented lynx occurrences in the Great Lakes region have been in the Mixed Deciduous/Coniferous Forest Province (Ruediger et al. 2002), where the forest canopy is dominated by white pine (*Pinus strobus*), red pine (*P. resinosa*), balsam fir (*Abies balsamea*), black spruce (*Picea mariana*), white spruce (*P. glauca*), northern white cedar (*Thuja occidentalis*), tamarack (*Larix laricina*), aspen (*Populus tremuloides*), and paper birch (*Betula papyrifera*). Canada lynx prey primarily on snowshoe hare (*Lepus americanus)*, which accounts for 35-97% of their diet (Kohler and Aubrey 1994). Other prey in the Great Lakes region include red squirrel (*Tamiasciurus hudsonicus*), flying squirrel (*Glaucomys sabrinus*), grouse (*Bonasa umbellus* and *Falcipennis canadensis*), beaver (*Castor canadensis*), mice (*Peromyscus* spp.), voles (*Microtus* spp.), and white-tailed deer (*Odocoileus virginianus*), though lynx are more likely to scavenge deer carcasses than to kill one on their own.

Lynx breeding activity peaks in March, resulting in a litter of up to five young, born 63-70 days later. Female lynx will breed during their first year when snowshoe hare are abundant, but otherwise wait until their second year (Quinn and Parker 1987). Males apparently do not breed in their first year (McCord and Cardoza 1982). Very few, if any, live kittens are born during lows in the snowshoe hare cycle (Brand and Keith 1979), but during years of snowshoe hare abundance the litter size can average four or five (Mowat et al. 1996).

Lynx density is highly dependent on the snowshoe hare cycle. The snowshoe hare literature suggests that southern populations of hare are cyclic, but at a lower amplitude than more northerly populations (Hodges 2000). Perhaps as a consequence, lynx home range size in the southern portions of the range tend to be larger (for females, more than twice as large on average) than those reported from more northerly areas, regardless of snowshoe hare abundance (Aubrey et al. 2000). However, lynx home range size can be highly variable. In Minnesota, two female home ranges were 51 km^2 and 122 km^2 (20 and 47 mi^2) (Mech 1980).

Because lynx are strongly dependent on snowshoe hare, their populations increase and then decline in response to the 7-10 year snowshoe hare cycle (Ward and Krebs 1985; O'Donoghue et al. 1998). Ward and Krebs (1985) documented minimum daily dispersal movements of 1.7 to 8.3 km (1 to 5 mi) per day. During lows in the snowshoe hare cycle, lynx have moved back and forth between Canada and the northern forested regions of the contiguous United States. One such movement between Ontario and Minnesota exceeded 1,000 km (600 mi) (Mech 1977).

Figure 5. Adult Canada lynx showing the characteristic long legs, large paws, ear tufts, and cheek whiskers. Photo courtesy of the Natural Resources Research Institute and the U.S. Forest Service.

In the early 1960s and again in the early 1970s significant numbers of lynx invaded northern Minnesota from Ontario, Canada (Mech 1973, 1980). These invasions were reflected in Canadian and MNDNR harvest records, which showed substantial peaks in harvest during the early 1960s and early 1970s (Figure 2). Again in the early 1980s, the Canadian provinces showed a significant high in lynx harvest; however, especially in Minnesota, the harvest was lower than the previous two decadal highs. A total of 57 lynx were taken from 1980 to 1984, with a high of 23 harvested during the winter of 1982-83 (Bill Berg, MNDNR unpublished data). Because of this low in harvest, Canada lynx were listed as a protected species in Minnesota in 1984, and by the mid-1990s they were presumed extirpated from the state. MNDNR has maintained that the lynx population in the state was never self-sustaining. McKelvey et al. (2000) found that historical records from the Lakes States, particularly from the 1960s and 1970s, were highly correlated with lynx population peaks in Canada and not with local hare population cycles. Although this does not rule out the persistence of local populations in the Lakes States, it supports the contention that population increases are primarily Canadian in origin. Nonetheless, between 1930 and 1984 there have been only a few years when lynx were not harvested, even during lows in the population cycle.

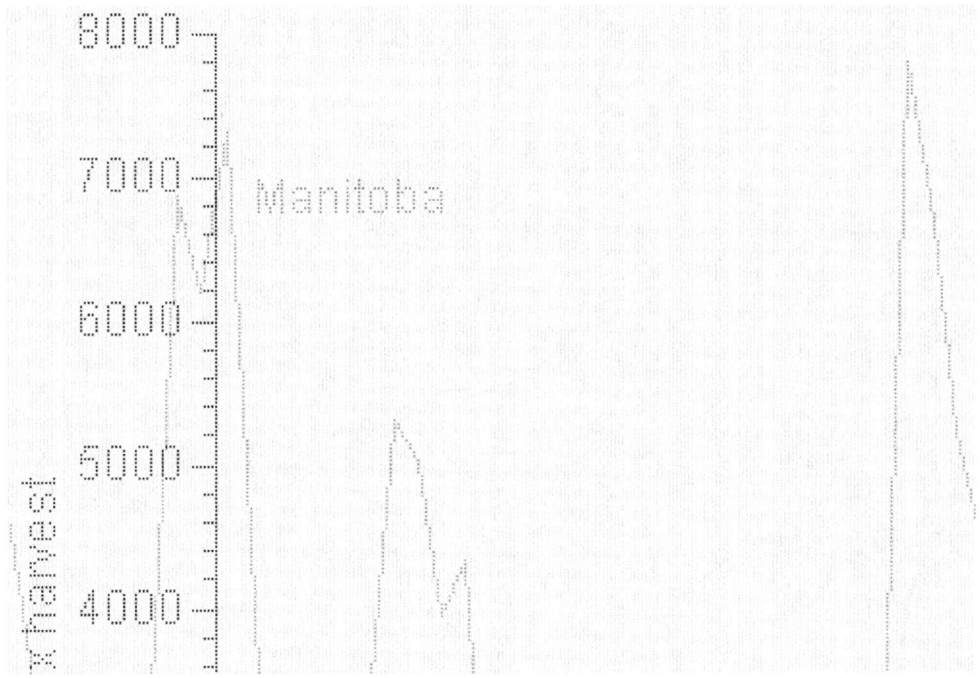

Figure 6. Lynx harvest records from Manitoba and Ontario, Canada, and the state of Minnesota. Legal harvest ended in Minnesota after 1984, when lynx were listed as state-threatened.

NPS D-166, February 2009